Librarians LOL

An Alphabet Soup Bowl in a Book of A- Z Poetic Inspirations for Teachers

Jeanine Jones

Speak To Me

Speak To Me Books
Memphis, TN

Librarians LOL
An Alphabet Soup Bowl in a Book of A-Z Poetic
Inspirations for Teachers: Volume 3

Paperback ISBN: 978-0-9884394-5-0
E-book ISBN: 978-0-9884394-6-7

Credits: Library Information Standards 1-4 are from the Shelby
County Schools Teacher Effectiveness Measurement Tool

Cover Design: Tywebbin Creations

DEDICATION

For
All School Librarians who find humor in a job they
take very seriously.

Especially,
the Library Information Specialists who have
inspired me along my journey as librarian, Alice
Faye Duncan, Stephanie Edwards, Joan Harvey,
Nancy Weathers and lastly, Yvonne Williamson.

ACKNOWLEDGEMENTS

Thank you, God, for allowing me to express myself poetically. Thank you, Marcus, my husband and biggest cheerleader for believing in me, being patient and always taking care of home. My children, I thank you for riding along with me on this journey. Also, I acknowledge and am thankful for Tomeka Frazier and Marcie Ivy for mailing me study packets in my educational quest to become a certified Library Information Specialist. Alice Faye Duncan, Stephanie Edwards, Joan Harvey, Nancy Weathers and lastly, but never least, Yvonne Williamson, THANK YOU! Your librarianship has helped me grow professionally. I appreciate you all welcoming me into the sisterhood of a profession that is vital for information access.

CONTENTS

Librarians Live, Love, and Laugh Through It All

The night before the first day of school you dreamed you heard this on the announcements "Good Morning Librarians! Today is the first day of 180. We can do this!" And you can. Just remember everything you learned in Laminating 101 and you'll be fine.

After several days of teaching that there is no such person, place or thing as a liberry, liberrian, or liberry teacher (*pick your flavor*), assisting with printing, laminating, removing fines, lunch duty, hall duty, teaching classes...and multitasking like no other in education, you survive your first week of the school year. You think, 5 days down 175 to go. You think about all you have to do and get your brims ready for your "berry" many tasks.

By the third Monday into the school year, hopefully, someone realizes you do more than check out books, and that you didn't study this task in school. It just comes with the job. Or you can just allow them to keep *ECLIPSing* your intelligence, smile, scan, and say "enjoy your book". Perhaps someone will say thank you. Either way, you push to enjoy and make the most your day. Surely it should be as great as you are!

However, by the fourth Monday of the school year, you're saying to yourself, "hang in there self."

Don't let the multi-grade level lesson plan, multi-subject, multi-everything shake you. Remind your colleagues that you are there to collaborate and assist, not to be the T.A. Walk in your greatness. You're the Library Information Specialist, L.I.S first, then a Library Media Specialist, L.M.S: Although, L.I.S is often confused with standing for Library Inventory Specialist or reduced to less. Yes L.E.S, exchanged for Library Equipment Specialist, L.E.S. Remind your colleagues that all things software and hardware should be referred to the I.T. help desk and that equipment falls under the department of Asset Management and Inventory Control. In between your cataloging, book blogging and making resources and information accessible, pay attention to your mental note of *why you went to school*. Remember that librarians are educators too and continue to have a *Happy Monday thru Friday* the rest of the school year despite the demands.

Embrace every break, holiday and mental health day. Celebrate those four-day weeks. Woo hoo! Make it to Labor Day! Cheer on the first official holiday of the school year. By this time, I know you are probably thinking about extending the break, resigning or retiring. Don't pack up and run for the border or back to the classroom just yet, you might just hit a wall (*you know they are building them*). Fall break is just around the corner. "You've got this!" Encourage yourself. The good book says "To whom much is given, much is required" *Luke12:48*. You were given the hub of the school. Stay connected. Tap into whatever source that keeps you fruitful.

As the school year keeps coming at you full throttle speed, you adjust. In the midst of checking out materials, finding docu-cams, cameras, projectors, bulbs, NWEA MAP testing, Achieve 3000 testing, or whatever testing your district uses, teaching, printing, copying, laminating etc... and keeping your head on straight; Hold fast to your goal. DISMISSAL! Hooray you get to leave, find your sanity, and come back tomorrow to do it all again. How fun! Remember you are the Queen of Multitasking. In some cases, King. Keep specializing in everything. One day you'll master something, perhaps, your crazy schedule of spontaneous requests.

On your journey remember, Librarians live out loud, love out loud, and laugh out loud through books, stories and literature. *Librarians Laugh Out Loud* is a place where Library Information Specialists a.k.a educators (*funny huh*), can laugh with others of the librarian species. Librarians laugh out loud, walking by faith in spaces that are often filled with the darkness of illiteracy, more so than the illuminating path of literacy.

Remember, support teachers are degreed, certified and then some. They have a specialty and, in most cases, have taught general education. Librarians you are more! You are the foundation. Most of all remember, Librarians are seriously funny people. You'd have to be one to know one.

Meanwhile, throughout the school year, periodically, sip on *Librarians Laugh out Loud*, a heartfelt, humorous Alphabet Soup Bowl in a Book, cooked up just for you in one big poetic pot of a greeting card, if you will, to inspire you on your journey. Enjoy it!

Have a great school year!

Jeanine Jones
#keepbookn'

3

Librarian, An Acrostic

Librarians an Extended Acrostic Introduction

Leader...

As a leader in literacy
Generally, librarians want everyone
in the building to read
Not just know how to read, but to read
Unfortunately, everyone will not follow the leader
However, you continue to lead by example
Creating books clubs, surveys, challenges
trivia and programs

Intellectual....

Continuously studying all kinds
of literature and media
sharing and conversing with others
at least a snippet of all that you find

pulling questions out of your
big red and white striped hat
that makes others think
you often fill the missing link

digging deep into the likes of your
Vaudeville Days, Dr. Seuss hat
you could have an app with funny little sayings
and nonsense raps
that actually make since
to the intellectual
and not so intellectual

perhaps, your highbrow above those pointy little
librarian glasses
are at attention for a reason
you are scholarly and intellectual
appealing to little intellects

even though you clown and costume around in humor
amuse them face
the best thing is that
you have all the information
and know all the right books
to check out

Brainiac...

Too smart for your own good
helping others as you should
brainiac in your own right
shedding *Information Power* and light
the super hero of the library
beware of the braniac librarian
she's coming to a school near you

Resourceful...

You have everything you need to know
at the tips of your fingers
in the confines of your library
not quite all knowing, like God
but you know where the good books are
other than the bible

Accessible...

Always available to help
all that dare to enter the literary garden
information
waiting
ready
accessible for the teachable
knowledge handy, seek-able
open and reachable
for all that dare grab it

Reliable Researcher...

From search engines, to .coms
to .govs, to .nets, to .orgs
you have connected all the dots
knowing all the right spots
to get good reliable information
from blogs to wikis
you are a very picky
regarding the research and source of choice

Inimitable...

Everyone in the building wants to know
what it is like to be the librarian
even if they think you only check out books
they want to scan and check out books too
your uniqueness is unmatched
incomparable to all the highly educated
non-book checkers in the building
they want to do what you do
even when they have no clue
you are inimitable
that's why per building, there's usually only one of you

Assiduous...

Diligent, constant and assiduous
hard working
book checking
persevering librarian
tirelessly working
in the name of literacy
energetically hustling and bustling books
actively and industriously
maintaining the livelihood and industry of
librarianship

Narrators ...

Telling stories
is how you thrive
rating plots, themes, and morals of stories
at story time

it is the listener's imagination
that you drive
into wanting to read and tell stories
just like you

with enthusiasm
suspense
and excitement
content and enriched too
little ones become readers
and narrators just like you

A-M Librarian
Laugh Out Loud
Poetic Inspirations

Astute...

Of good judgment librarians are heaven sent
cleverly dispelling stupidity and ignorance incisively
astutely advising the not so eager to learn
and the eager to learn
positively and perceptively

making the smart and not so smart smarter
and empowered with resources
tools
knowledge and data bases
to tackle their toughest
social and academic cases

Bookworm...

Librarians are bookworms at best
bibliophiles, avid readers, book lovers
most days your head is in book
deciphering or enjoying fiction or nonfiction

until one day
reading the shelves
you discover that you're not the only bookworm
and that bookworms are real bugs

you see them in the literal form of silverfish
you throw the book
give a second glance
and compose yourself
you now understand the term
more than figuratively

bookworms live in books
feeding of words and papyrus

Collaborate...

Working together to join forces
providing excellent literary reading choices

you collaborate
teaming up in partnerships
with schools and communities
seeking grants
for literacy and technology

although you buy a lot of books
that often times just sit pretty on the shelves
you make the budget
meet deadlines
and supply literary wealth

Dust...

Collecting more than books
you acquire just as much dust in your library as books
powdered sprinkles of dust fly from the shelves
of covered literature
trying to mask the message

dusting the mask away
as you clean underneath the grime, filth and dirt
the dust clears
and you find powerful words
that young minds need to hear

you dust off the book and put it on display
hoping some reader will check it out
in the near future
or at least some day

Expert...

An expert at ordering collections
assessing fines
online public access catalogs
managing programs

skilled at catering to supply and demand
proficient in all things liberry, library
and not so library
especially the highly acclaimed story time
you are a professional
an adept, well maintained
library information specialist
frazzled hair and all

you get the job done
your special set of skills
your expertise is often utilized

Finder...

Finder of all knowledge
from Dusable to Vespucci
even the great discoverer Dora the Explorer
you become book detective
spotter
identifier of the page-turner
detecting readers
and non-readers
inspecting books
finding culprits
who disrespects books
teaching them how to respect literacy
literature
and the package and form
that they come in
finally, locating and leading
the new reader
to a new world of literacy

Generous...

Always giving information
and service with a smile
to everyone
like a fast food worker
even the fake smile
that comes along with the job

you know that generosity is the key
generously helping in the fight
to combat illiteracy
you keep giving
all that you have
so that others
will have
what no one can take away

Helpful...

Helping out with everything
in the school
and everyone
in the school
you are the go to person
go figure
since everyone thinks you just check out books
in times of need
suddenly, you become the guru
of all things unknown to others
even if you don't know how to help initially
you find a way to make sure the seeker finds
what he needs

Insightful...

Sharing insight on all topics imaginable
you've broken into the librarian's code
haphazardly
you've read at least one book
from each section of Dewey
giving more insight
and the right of reading passage
foreseen to some, but at first sight blind to others

Job Description Clarity
(Poetic Sermon)

Hello. hello, hello educators
I'm not sure if you know what School Library
Information Specialist really do
Some of you do, but so many don't
So I just want to take this time to clarify,
because being back into the first week of school with
in-service and PD and all
Every year it seems to get a little confusing as to what
we, librarians really do
So I just want to clear it up

We need our colleagues and paraprofessionals to
know that we too, hold degrees and certifications for
the position that we hold

I know
It's hard to believe
But nowhere in our curriculum or program of Library
Science study did we study Laminating 101
I'm just bringing that up because I must've laminated
about three hundred items the first week of school
alone, before the students returned
Two hundred of those items were done on a Friday
and I was just like kind of confused as to what I
should be doing, with all that I'm really supposed to
be doing, and wondering how I will do it...

You know, provide resources school-wide, collaborate
with other educators and you know, just service the
whole community

But this is what happens when people think that you
just check out books,
check out and inventory equipment,
which is not even a part of a librarian's job
description
do story time and recite *Mother Goose* rhymes

Nowhere in our education were these things the
primary topic
You know an assistant can check out books, and you
know other children can read a story to another child
I need you to look at it like this my fellow colleagues
See if your specialty is English, Math, Science,
History, Spanish, French, Music,
Theatre or Dance etc.
Ours is Library Science and we were assigned
equipment inventory
just like you could have been the administrator's pick
Sure the librarian is always happy to, or at least act
like she is happy to do it when it comes to assisting in
all of those areas

However, we actually have to design a plan and
adhere to a budget to provide resources for the entire
school community
Meaning that...
We have to be knowledgeable of the curriculum across
the board
We need to know what's going on in every discipline
We need to support Common Core

We are not the computer techs

We did not study that
We did not study computer science
We do not know how to fix your computer
We are not the ones to call to hook up computers

but, I'm quite sure there's a helpdesk number in your
district that you can call and it can probably even be
done online if teachers would inbox, email,
or simply ask
We would be more than happy
at least in appearance to show you the way
IT is the answer!

Anyway,
I just want to welcome everybody back into the school
year as usual
and assure you that it's going to be a great year
I'm going to be touching base with you periodically
to see how it's going
Making sure everyone knows what it is that library
information specialists does

You know, you know, you know we wear a lot of hats,
and juggle a lot of things and just want others to
understand what we're supposed to do

but we're very, very happy to help with all the things
that are so often asked of us

Now as a library information specialist I know
I will be laminating and doing those type of things and
de-cluttering areas that I have no idea where the
things go
But if you've seen my garage
that's, that's one thing

If you saw my garage you would not asked me to
organize a space or de-clutter anything

I am capable of organizing the space
but let me find out where everything is first
Then we can work from there

I cannot check you out of docu-camera or a projector
when I have no idea where the things are myself
I need to, to develop a system
Get my space together as well for when I receive the
children
Remember I serve all of the students in the entire
school
and my planning becomes a period where I assist you
but this is just all in fun and all in love and
understanding
just bringing a little clarity as to what Library
Information Specialists do
You take it all in fun and
in love, peace and understanding of what we actually
do

Seriously,

According to our evaluation rubric, library
information specialists are to
provide Instruction,
teach students to inquire,
think critically and gain knowledge,
draw inclusions,
make informed decisions,
apply knowledge to new situations and
create new knowledge

Provide environment space, resources and routines

with Professionalism, developing programmatic
growth

Hopefully, you now have clarity
or at least an idea of
the Job description of a Library Information Specialist

Keeper...

Keeper of books
kids
student sit-ins
babysitting books
and students
keeper of the utmost importance
knowledge and power
keys to unlock so much information
and chance
you are a great steward

Librarians Laugh Out Loud...

Librarians laugh out loud,
love out loud
and live out loud

through books, stories and literature
authors styles, plots and themes
limericks and characters

they tell and retell stories
for all to get the moral

finding the humor in a variety of things
not just in printed stories
they laugh at the daily librarian realities

like teachers not caring
about the classification of Dewey
a decimal point system designed to organize and
guide
instead of using it, they prefer the librarian to go look
and find
whatever it is they need

students not caring about checking out a book
until it is time for them to do an assignment
not caring about turning it in

until their report card or diploma
is withheld from them
not seeing the need to own a public library card
thinking more choices make the work hard

Librarians laugh out loud about die-hard readers
who reverse the norm
that reader that checks out
300 to 400-page books daily

then returns them the next day
requesting more of the same
something similar to read, aye
you remember this kid's name
his schedule
and find other kids like him
to start a book club
with other kids who like to read just as much

Librarians laugh out loud and are sarcastically thrilled
when they have to teach basic elementary library skills
to middle and high school scholars
who by the lack of knowledge, seem unbothered

Librarians laugh out loud
at teachers same day requests
for presentations on plagiarism, research projects
and multiple classroom book sets

lamination, copies, and inventory deadlines
substitute teaching
and unpaid book fines

watching vocational students
until the dismissal bell rings
Librarians laugh out loud at all these things

they really crack up
when teachers see them as their assistant
and not as a colleague of knowledge, assistance and
expertise

Librarians laugh out loud even harder
at the looks on their colleagues faces
when they finally lay down the library law and take a
stance
to nicely put them in their places

seriously, librarians laugh out loud
to keep from crying
about students neglect, disregard and disrespect
for books knowledge and information

the thousands of dollars spent per scholar
for materials and resources
to build a quality collection for education
that will never be absorbed
because their minds are absorbed
with sound bites from uninformed lips
and social media writers

so, to keep it not a sad, but humorous trip...

Librarians laugh out loud at being called lie-berry-ans
instead of librarians
and when someone says their going to the lie-berry
instead of the library

as they gently remind
there are black berries
blueberries
raspberries

strawberries
and even cranberries
but there are no lie-berries
or lie-berryans

Librarians laugh out loud
love out loud
and live out loud
through books stories and literature
authors styles, plots themes
limericks and characters
and library realities

Memory...

Your memory is somewhat like an elephant

You remember...

Where things are, past eras
Who checked out what
What teacher or student is usually in a funk
and what magic it takes to cheer them up

What books readers like
Who likes to write
Who likes to read
Who frequents the library
if only for technology

What teachers support
What students smart alecky retort
from generalities to biographies
you have a great memory

N-Z Librarians
Laugh Out Loud
Poetic Inspirations

Numbers...

Dealing with Dewey and inventory
and invented scanner counting systems
call numbers, serial numbers and district assigned
equipment numbers

you fill like a numbers runner or lotto announcer
for the enormous amount of numbers you deal with
and you could probably do with or without math
but numbers are in your every task
from ordering, to shelving
from checking out, to checking in
you're a book person
but numbers made themselves your friends
when you decided to be a librarian

Overseer...

Overseer of books, technology
you watch entrances and exits
book drops
computers and computer carts
ipads and laptops

overseeing everything in your Literary Garden
from circulation to teacher stations
you watch to see if a book will grow a tree of readers
in that sacred space
they call the lie-berry

Powerful...

Information Power
is where you got your start
to librarianship
you use that information
to take others on a powerful trip
to the literary garden
into places they've never heard of
learning things they never dreamed of
you are powerful and in the know
eager to watch readers grow

Quiet...

Shhh!
Someone's reading a book
Keep quiet!
You exclaim and command
Starting a *shhhshing* riot

"BE Quiet" in your best whispering voice

the children continue

"That lady evil" the children say
"Crazy"
"Book villain" they say
"We don't do anything fun"
"Coming to the library boring"

You let them talk
Work in groups
They get too loud

"Oops!"
The *shhhshing* game begins again

"That lady evil"
the children say
"Crazy"
"Book villain"
they say
"She gon' make us read all day"

"Y'all be quiet"
"We don't do anything fun"
"Coming to the library boring"

Rich...

If you have an office
then you probably have paper cups, paper plates
paper napkins, paper towels and any other paper
except for cash

somewhere in your library, you have a stash....
of color paper, designer paper, school letterhead
paper, boarder paper
freeze paper, bulletin board paper, news papers
and the most requested
print paper

libraries are filled will so many rich resources
mostly in printed book form
in addition to paper, paper, paper ...
you have scarlet letters, magazines, atlases and
inventory lists,
so much paper, enough to restart the Chicago fire

you admire the thought of going digital
but love the richness of the printed book
and the enriching experience it gives
you want the beautiful trees live
and they do...

at Forest Library,
there, they're reincarnated
their spirits live

woods filled with enough books
for all to read
boldly placed, daring someone to read them, take a
walk on the wild side
grab a taste of knowledge
go for it
succeed

encouraging all to just
Read, Read, Read
it's free dried fruit
from the recycled tree of knowledge
the best fruit of life
Literacy
edible only figuratively
food for thought, literally

there shouldn't be a hungry person
with all these liberries
or a poor person
with all these libraries

Sanctuary...

Peace, quiet, calm and soothing
like the Methodist or Catholic Church
the library becomes the sanctuary

some people come to be refilled
even those not religious or spiritual
worship books
and quench their thirst for knowledge

through book studies, book signings
the literary baptizing
takes place, converting nonreaders into readers
and thinkers about the printed word
and writers of the work

Trustworthy...

Librarians are trustworthy
giving advice like bartenders and bank lenders
the only return they expect
is a satisfied loyal customer
who attends the book bar often

leaving so inebriated
with useful information
hooked on a genre
sedated by an author's style
engulfed by a series
readers, seekers getting high off the free supply

Smashed off words

your recommendations are reliable resources
and often times not a bad vice
but great book choices
you are the book pusher
trusted for good products

hopefully,
everyone will try them

Uber...

Uber in your service
and professionalism
you give others a lift
driving knowledge
delivering it to all
leading others in the direction that they need to go, to
grow
uniquely arriving right on time
with what's needed
steering paths to higher places

Vocabulary...

Words on the wall
to increase library skills
vendor terms, jargon, vocabulary drills
lexiles, lexicon, synonyms and antonyms
use of the thesaurus, vocabulary lists
and new spelling words
challenging scholars to use the new words they've
heard

Write...

In collaboration with students, you encourage
students to read, read, read and write
They reply:

Poetry, Drama, Fiction, Non Fiction
All about somebody else's life and my diction
Novels, plays, short stories, essays
Who cares to read, write them anyway

Assessment writing, nail biting
Pre and Post writing
It's just not exciting

Quick writes causes mares of night and fluency's no
friend of mine
Transitions are my disposition and let's not mention
revisions
Revising and editing despise me
But reading and writing I must do so teach me
something
something new

I like Hip-Hop!
Can't you see
but you just teach poetry

If I could make a hyperbole plea
Then maybe you'll see
that Hip-Hop is the thing

47

Rap, it's rhythm and poetry
and the beats make it interesting
So, teach me Hip-Hop through Reading and Writing
If I must do what's challenging to me
May it be just as challenging to you, to make it
exciting
To do something you don't like to
Do something new
To get me to do something you want me to do
To get me to read and write

So, teacher, teacher will you please integrate rhythm
and poetry
into the lesson
I promise I'll learn and have good diction
I'll apply my skills to drama, fiction and nonfiction
I'll watch for similes and metaphors and have fun with
word wars

I'll Read
I'll Write

X-Factor...

You know what others don't
the unknown is in your library
accessible to all who care to find out
solving for x is your daily agenda
even though you're not teaching Algebra
or working with numbers
you possess the x-factor

Ying-Yang...

Books everywhere
here and there
it's the end of the year
inventory is near
a librarian meltdown
is closer than it appears
books out of place
on shelves
carts
podium stands
and the circulation desk
books coming out of the ying-yang
and you're just trying to hang
hang in there
until they're all scanned, weeded and/or discarded
or until the last day
whichever comes first

Zing...

You added zing in everything
from day one
you put in time, work and energy
giving the same vitality of literacy
creating an alphabet soup bowl in the form of books
for all to enjoy, create and learn from
packing a powerful punch
to all that entered the literary garden
adding vigor and life in the form of a smile, printed
word
paperback, hardbound or digital book
Zing-ing-ly, laughing out loud
as a librarian
you give life, love and laughs through books, stories
and literature

Thank you for reading.

Read all the books in the...
An Alphabet Soup Bowl in a Book Series

When All God's Teachers Get To Heaven

God's Special Educators are Teachers Too

Librarians LOL

Teachers LOL

Doing 180 Days to Life

ABOUT THE AUTHOR

Jeanine Jones, born Jeanine Books, is a native of Chicago, Illinois. As an educator in an urban school system, she is responsible for educating youth who are challenged in the areas of academics and socio-economics. Cultural development, the arts and literacy are important factors in her work. She is continuously striving to develop new strategies that are effective for struggling readers. Her absolute affinity for literature, especially poetry, propels her to teach and constantly learn. As a spoken-word artist, poet, and creative writer, Arts Integration is an essential component of her practice. She attributes her early love of reading and the arts to her parents. They made it possible for her to experience and live life creatively.

"Literacy is Life~ Live!" is her motto.

www.ingramcontent.com/pod-product-compliance
Lightning Source LLC
Chambersburg PA
CBHW070800050426
42452CB00012B/2424